The Roof Don't Leak:

Thoughts, Reflections and Wisdom

By

Tommie "Ttop" Rivers

Edited by
Sonya Carey, M.S.
and
Debra Warner, Psy.D.

Published by SCRIPT

SCRIPT
ISBN 979-8-218-22503-2

Printed in the United States
1st Printing 2023

ATTENTION: ORGANIZATIONS & CORPORATIONS
Bulk quantity discounts for reselling, gifts or fundraising are available. For more information, please contact Script stopthestigma.scriptconference@gmail.com

Cover Design: Dave Warner

*To my children, Keyun, Nyla and Zuri.
All I do, I do for you.*

*To my Mom, Gwen, the woman who gave me life
and taught me basic instructions before leaving this
earth. You are my everything.*

*To Momma Hayes, the woman who took me in as
her own. Thank you and rest in peace.*

*To my sisters Angela, Meme and Tara and my
brothers Rob and Tommy Lee.*

To my sister Nita, rest in peace.

To my nieces, nephews, and grandchildren.

Acknowledgments

Special thanks to Tony Nicholas, Bo Taylor, Scot Obler, and Aquil Basheer.

Rest in Peace, Jim Brown and James Ingram.

Thanks to "Doc" for getting this on the page and to Sonya for her vision.

My PCITI team members. Rest in Peace, Brenda Hubbard.

A special thanks to my sister, Angela, and brothers Rob, Tara and Tommie. Rest in peace, my sister Nita.

Thank you to Amanda, Dione and Ruth.

Much love to my family in Nashville and Chattanooga, Tennessee, my tribe the Geers.

Last but not least, I give thanks to my heavenly and earthly fathers. My heavenly father, who taught me unconditional love and forgiveness, and my earthly father, who taught me how to be a father by his absence. They also had to communicate across all divides and cultures.

Table of Contents

Foreword

By Debra Warner, Psy.D.

This book is the second time in my career that I have felt completely proud of my relationship with the community. This book embodies the role that I believe God destined for me: to help and support others in their life journeys to find self-empowerment and fulfill their purpose.

When I met Tommie "Ttop," he didn't judge me. He allowed this psychologist, who knew nothing about his world, to understand it from his perspective. That takes an inner strength and vulnerability few people have. When you come across someone with those qualities, you know you have to listen to them for they will stir your soul. That's why I have chosen to share Tommie Ttop's journey.

I encourage those who pick up this book not just to read Ttop's words, but to listen to the meaning and experience behind them. Then I challenge you to go into your community and embody that same spirit to create change. By knowing Tommie Ttop, I realized I was a change agent just by my willingness to try.

Introduction: Dreams and Aspirations

When I was younger, I played baseball and football despite being surrounded by negative influences. At that time, I dreamed of becoming a professional baseball player and buying a big house. I often shared these aspirations with my mother and thought it was my only path to success.

Then, I fell into the gang culture and lifestyle, and my dream became clouded by darkness. I want to shed light on the part of the game many people don't understand, the twisted thinking and mentality that comes with that lifestyle.

As a young kid in the gang culture, my biggest aspiration was to go to jail, lift weights, and come out with a lot of respect. It was a self-fulfilling prophecy I didn't even realize at the time. It's important to be careful what you wish for in our communities. Even in sports, I always strived to be the best. Unfortunately, being the best meant something entirely different in the gang culture. My goals and aspirations have drastically changed since then.

I aspire to be a stand-up guy and be there for my kids and family daily. I want to run a successful business without constantly looking over my shoulder. It's a blessing to be able to strive toward being a profound author or the top motivational speaker in the country. I want to be a beacon of light and hope for our people, culture, and community. I want to be someone who is remembered for standing up for change.

I aspire to be great like the pioneers who sacrificed before us: Malcolm X, Martin Luther King Jr., Nat Turner, and other unspoken forces who fought for our people. People like Tony Nicholas and James Ingram were instrumental in my life. I want to be someone who helps others on their journey, someone who people can look back on and say, "He helped me."

I know I could be better, and I still face daily challenges. I believe that we will face situations we can't control every day, and we need to let God handle those things and focus on what we can control.

Part 1: The Gang Lifestyle

In Reflection

As a child growing up in a community where most of my friends came from gang culture, that lifestyle of being the dressed the best, having the prettiest girls, and being the toughest guy was very tempting. The lifestyle looked good on the outside. The shell of it looked beautiful.

I'm going to give you some good and some bad from it. I've reached the highest level of gangbanging. I'll tell you the truth about it. *There is no retirement plan, no 401k. The only thing we see from the lifestyle is death, destruction, the killing of our people, and the devaluation of us as human beings.*

I look at the struggles our ancestors went through to get us here, the battle to help us feel equal to the person next to us. As I've gone through that lifestyle, I have a duty now to tell my people and my community that there is nothing good about joining a gang. I gained family but also enemies in that process. So, to you and those who think the lifestyle is good, it's not.

So much of society views our community as thugs and gangsters. The news, television shows, and movies talk about our kids dealing drugs, shooting guns, killing. The media glamorizes the lifestyle. All of this is a mirage. Nothing from the lifestyle is productive for us in this day and age. So many individuals, including myself, have gone through that lifestyle and are now returning to our communities and telling the truth about it.

I grew up in the eighties when dudes were rapping about the lifestyle. I lived it, and I will not sit here and act like it's cool for the youth. Glamourizing gang culture means we are setting our kids up for failure. We are no different than the Ku Klux Klan.

If we say that our lives matter, we have to set the standard on what we want people to respect about us as human beings. How can we ask people to respect us when we don't respect ourselves? We must respect our neighbors, grandparents, aunties, uncles, nieces and nephews, mom and dad. We have to return to normality and stop looking at individuals like they are our enemies. That is a culture where we are taught to be hardcore, to walk past the next brother or sister with our noses turned up and fists clenched.

The frown ain't nothing but a smile turned upside down, right? We can change the output with new input. We've been tricked. Now it is up to us to tell the truth. These young cats talk about how they like the gang lifestyle and that culture. Still, they will tell everything as soon as they are handcuffed and removed from their families. So why put yourself in that situation? Get a job. Surround yourself with people that can get you jobs. There are people out there who can help us while still fighting an uphill battle of their own.

Let me make everybody understand that there is hope. Some people can help get us into positions to grow. Make sure that you're not silent. Make sure that you know the people that God places around you. Don't be afraid to ask for help.

Remember, nothing from nothing leaves nothing. I'm my brother's keeper, not their mother's weeper. We are accountable for ourselves and our community.

Short-Time Glamor

I want to share the harsh reality of short-term glamour and long-term misery in the gang lifestyle. I was imprisoned as a teenager when I didn't fully comprehend who I was or my life's purpose. I was just sixteen when the case happened, seventeen when I was arrested , nineteen when I was sentenced. I served nine years and seven months for a crime I didn't commit. *The glamour and respect of belonging to a gang can be short-lived The consequences of getting caught can last a lifetime._*I learned this the hard way, standing up for my beliefs and my community and paying a high price for it.

So, when I look back at the couple of years, I spent living a harmful lifestyle, having nice cars and jewelry, it was just short-term glamor. But when I eventually got caught and went to jail, it resulted in long-term misery. We must ask ourselves if it's worth sacrificing many years of our own lives, or someone else's life, to build a false image in order to gain acceptance from our peers. It's like the blind leading the blind. We must understand that everything we do has consequences and weigh those consequences before making decisions. It's not worth it in the end.

We live in a fast-paced era where people crave instant gratification without considering sustainability or longevity. However, I have learned that slow and steady wins the race and that longevity should be our ultimate goal. We must build our lives with a strong foundation from the ground up, brick by brick, to ensure that we are unshakeable during times of crisis. It's like taking the stairs when the elevator is broken. We may have to go step by step, but we will get there in the end. Having something that lasts is worth the time and effort.

So, to achieve long-term success and avoid the consequences of short-term gratification, I've learned that building a solid foundation is important.

Building something from the top down with no foundation will crumble at the first sign of distress or change. Instead, I have learned to focus on building sustainable systems supporting my growth and longevity.

I often advise my friends who are still caught up in the lifestyle of quick cash and drugs that it's short-term glamor with long-term misery. They may make a lot of money in a year or two, but eventually, they will get caught and spend years in prison. So it's important to look beyond immediate gratification and focus on building a solid foundation for long-term success.

We need to change our thinking and understand that something that looks glamorous on the outside may not have any substance on the inside. We must consider whether it's worth our time and energy and also look to the legacy we want to leave for ourselves and our community.

How do we create generational wealth? It's not about immediate gratification but rather about longevity and sustainability. The name of the game is longevity, which requires building a foundation that can withstand times of crisis. We need to focus on constant growth and evolution, which only happens with a longevity mindset. Then, you get back what you put into the game.

Wrongly Convicted

Being falsely accused cost me ten years of my life. It's crazy to think that my involvement in gang culture and my decisions along the way led to such a huge loss. But at that time, I had no higher aspirations than to say I had been to prison, which is a sick way of thinking. I also didn't realize that I would actually fulfill that prophecy. *Changing our mindset and understanding that our choices have long-term consequences is important. We should strive for higher goals and aspirations that lead to a better future for ourselves and our communities.*

There is a significant gap in our system for young men who lack the economic means to afford proper legal representation. Public defenders, who handle hundreds of cases daily, often don't even know their clients' names and view them only as files rather than human beings. It's a heartbreaking reality. It's even more devastating for juveniles who are sent to prison.

To be tried as an adult when I was a minor was a harsh reality. Even now, decades later into adulthood, my record continues to hinder me from pursuing certain opportunities and fulfilling my purpose in life. It's discouraging and disheartening, but I remind myself that God has a plan for me and won't place me where I don't belong. Despite my record, I've dedicated my life to saving lives, being a positive influence, coaching football, and mentoring young athletes. I've enjoyed seeing some of my former students make it to the professional level. By God's grace, I built a sports camp that develops student-athletes and gives back to the community. My past does not define me, and I am grateful for the blessings I've received.

Being falsely accused and pleading guilty out of the belief that I had no other option created a heavy burden on my life, but I also recognize that my journey has led me to a place where I can lead, teach, and help others in similar situations.

There are no saints in the Bible who did not come from a prophecy of sin. The only thing I can control is my current work. I have chosen to use my experiences to make a positive impact. As a juvenile, I didn't fully understand the consequences of my actions or the weight of my aspirations. But now, I strive to create a legacy built on positive impact and meaningful contribution.

I fought my case for nearly three years. Looking back, I realized that God sent me on a journey of understanding. Once in prison, I immediately hit the books, educating myself and not taking on a victim's mentality. I returned home and positively changed my life, community, and the people around me.

I want to apologize to anyone I may have hurt along my journey, including my family and friends. I hope people see me for who I am now and what I have accomplished over the past thirty years. I have written three books and participated in three documentaries. I am working on my newest book, "Working in the Community to Effect Change."

I have learned to turn negatives into positives and want to encourage anyone going through struggling, including those falsely accused or convicted of a crime, to find people who can support and help them.

Accountability

Firstly, I want to emphasize the importance of accountability. Repenting and seeking forgiveness is crucial because we're all imperfect and make mistakes along the way. *It's essential to ask for forgiveness if we've harmed someone, no matter the situation or level of impact. Accountability is vital in any relationship or situation, and I hold myself responsible for my actions.* In terms of being wrongly accused, it has undoubtedly affected my family and personal growth. It was a challenging experience, and I had to fight my case for almost three years. However, God allowed me to go through this experience to teach me a lesson and help me grow.

I am not perfect, and I have made mistakes. I have prayed for forgiveness many days and nights from the depths of my soul. If there is anyone out there that I have hurt or harmed in any way, please forgive me. I must hold myself accountable and ask for forgiveness, especially from my days in the gang culture where I may have caused harm to others. Having a good heart has also saved my life regarding that lifestyle.

Being accountable and treating others with respect is important to me. However, being wrongly accused has been the worst experience for me. It feels like there is always a cloud over my head, and people who don't know me negatively perceive me. It's unfortunate how economics continue to affect our community. If I had the financial means, I wouldn't have had to face the charges that I did or plead guilty to a case that had nothing to do with me.

It's upsetting how little people know about their rights and the legal system. I was told that if I didn't plead guilty, I could face forty-six years to life in prison. It turned out that these were just lies to scare me into taking a plea deal. I have seen others also unfairly treated by the legal system It's disheartening to know how steep and how often the odds are stacked against us.

Sitting in jail for an extended period can make you desperate. I felt like the only way out was to take a plea bargain, even though I was innocent. It's unjust, but unfortunately, it's the reality of our legal system.

That conviction has held me back in many ways, from high-paying jobs to other opportunities that have come my way. The system knows what it's doing when it coerces us into taking plea deals. It's another way to get young Black men off the streets and further demonize us. It's a profoundly sad reality because my family, friends, and those close to me know who I am. They know the truth about me, yet the system is quick to label and judge without truly understanding or caring about its impact on our lives.

It's heartbreaking to think that in cases like mine, it wasn't just me who suffered. Five of us were caught up in the system. It's a tragic reality how the system targets and criminalizes Black men, locking us in prisons and treating us like animals, depraved and sick. When we're released, we're left with no resources or tools. All we have is the lingering weight of stigma that makes it near impossible to survive in a world that expects us to thrive despite all odds, especially in the face of gang life.

And they wonder why so many people are struggling with mental health and going down the wrong path. It's only by the grace of God that I haven't lost my mind and spiraled out of control. Anyone who has gone through what I have would struggle to survive, but I've managed to keep going. Sadly, many of my childhood friends are either dead or serving life sentences. It's a hard reality to face and still affects my kids today. But I refuse to give up. I must lead by example and keep pushing forward. Thankfully, I have a support system of good people who understand how the system works and know the truth. So here I am, being honest and vulnerable, trusting in God. I have no regrets about my journey.

Incarceration is Slavery
Prisons are nothing more than warehouses with human beings as livestock. While I was in jail, I spent a lot of time contemplating the history of slavery and how my people were brought to this country in chains and shackles on

ships. Fast forward to today, prisoners are transported in chains and shackles on buses that are the property of the state of California. Private investors run prisons and exploit the labor of prisoners, who are paid a measly 25 cents an hour to produce goods sold on the streets for exorbitant amounts of money. It's reminiscent of the sweatshops in third-world countries where workers are paid pennies on the dollar while others make millions off their labor. This is what I mean when I talk about livestock. We are treated like cattle, kept in confinement for years, told what to do and what not to do. Then, we produce the goods that they order us to make. It's a dehumanizing and exploitative system that needs to change.

Why do you think that the prison industry is more profitable than education? It's because every time a person is incarcerated, the system profits. Even the simple act of moving an inmate from one facility to another generates revenue. For example, when the sheriff's department transfers you from Wayside County Jail in northern Los Angeles County to the jail in downtown Los Angeles, they get paid for it. This is why people often get moved around without a court date to generate more profit for the system. It's all about economics. This is why there's so much suppression, and new private prisons are popping up. They make money off the body.

It is modern-day slavery at its finest. They have created systems that place us in prisons and then make money off us. It's mind-boggling that we don't fully grasp what's happening. We need to change our mindset and look hard at the issues in our society. We must recognize that this is happening in our culture. I've caught myself saying this before and had to pause to reflect on the gravity of it all.

Have you ever thought about this? So many look back at slavery and say, "If I was in that situation, I wouldn't have stood for it. They would have had to kill me." But the reality is it's still happening today. It's just been made to look more appealing. When you go to jail or prison, it's essentially the same as slavery. In the South, incarcerated people still work on plantations, shackled around their ankles. We need to wake up, recognize our people's conditions, and work to change them by voting and fighting for a new, better world.

Our society uses mothers whose sons have been victims of gang violence to speak out against progressive Los Angeles County District Attorney George Gascón. Some of these parents have children doing life sentences and say the penalties are too harsh. Why is that? Harsh sentencing laws, such as three strikes, result in individuals receiving lengthy sentences for non-violent crimes. Gascón is reversing the curse on this system; he's releasing those subjected to double or triple jeopardy. We need to understand what we're dealing with and what we're looking at. Instead, they want to use Gascón as a scapegoat, then bring someone with an iron fist back in place. Think about this: When it's your child you want mercy. When it's their child you want justice. We'll return to heavy suppression and double and triple jeopardy for our people. Pay attention to the systemic racism plaguing us unless you want your child to be the next piece of livestock in a human warehouse.

My Record

My criminal record has hindered my ability to obtain certain jobs. *This is especially difficult in my work, which involves engaging with populations such as gangs and tribes. It can be challenging for someone with a felony conviction to get hired in a role where they can make a meaningful impact and facilitate positive change.* Unfortunately, I believe that the system is designed to dehumanize and marginalize people like me with the use of things like the three-strikes law and other punitive measures that serve to perpetuate a cycle of imprisonment and disenfranchisement.

When it comes to finding employment, it can be discouraging for individuals with a criminal record. In many cases, we are faced with the reality of checking "yes" to a question asking if we have ever been convicted of a felony while others can check "no." Unfortunately, this simple question can decide whether we are even considered for the job. It's frustrating that the system is designed to keep us from moving forward and making positive changes in our lives.

When it comes to getting jobs, it's difficult for ex-felons to have a fair chance, especially in the work that involves dealing with the population we serve. Having a criminal record makes it hard for us to effect change and help our communities. For instance, if an employer is given two job applications, one from a person with a felony conviction and the other without, chances are the person without a record will be chosen.

Despite my achievements over the past twenty-five years, my criminal record hinders me from getting specific opportunities. It's frustrating because if someone else had done the same work, they would be praised as philanthropists and humanitarians and be up for many different things. But because of my record, I'm not given those chances. The system puts us in situations where we have to plead guilty or take deals we don't fully understand. It's up to us to trust in God to help us navigate through these challenges.

It's frustrating how the system limits our opportunities and obstructs our progress. For example, public defenders unfamiliar with our cases make deals with district attorneys for their own benefit, so they don't have to put in the work of going to trial, but even though that may not be to the benefit of their clients. It's disheartening how the system works against us and hinders our growth as a community. However, we must acknowledge that there are laws in place that affect everyone negatively, not just our community.

Every individual's story is unique, and it's important to understand that. However, the current system categorizes people with criminal records as if they're all the same and doesn't give them a chance to grow. It's like they put a shell around us to prevent us from being a threat to society, businesses, and humanity. It's interesting to note that many successful people in our society also have asterisk marks next to their names. This cannot be a coincidence and suggests that this system is designed for a reason.

So, here we are again, facing the same issues that have plagued our ancestors for generations. We must look at each person individually and find a way for the system to see us as human beings with unique stories and experiences rather than simply labeling and categorizing us. We need a reevaluation of how things are done to move toward a more just and equitable society.

The Soil Beneath My Feet

Adjusting to being different in the real world can be a challenge. When I returned home from prison, I noticed that many things remained unchanged. While there were superficial differences in fashion and style, it was disheartening to see that so much remained the same. My mindset had shifted, and I was focused on personal growth and evolution. My motivation was to provide for my family and be a responsible member of society.

However, the adjustment can be challenging. You may experience shell shock. Even the sound of cars backfiring can trigger memories of gunshots and lead to Posttraumatic Stress Disorder. Additionally, the pace of society outside can feel overwhelming after the slow, steady routine of prison life. Incarceration offers a unique opportunity for introspection and self-reflection without the outside world's distractions. However, the distractions of daily life can make it challenging to stay focused and on track. This adjustment shocked me, and I imagine it was the same for many others.

On the other hand, my mental fortitude was incredibly strong, and I was determined not to let anyone or anything lead me back to prison. When I was released, a prison guard told me he would see me back soon. That comment motivated me to never return, and I used my negative experiences to fuel growth. I refused to let others' opinions hinder my progress, recognizing that everyone has their own perspective. The challenges I faced upon release were mainly related to adjusting to the outside world. I am blessed to say that my journey has been guided by God.

When I first came home, I started working at Macy's, putting sensors on clothes for four hours a night. From there, I worked my way up to assistant dock manager and eventually to dock manager. After leaving Macy's, I was asked to be the logistics manager and trained other dock managers across the company. I was even in charge of hiring and firing at Macy's and hired ten of my friends and associates. Unfortunately, they were all let go due to background checks.

It's important to note that I secured a job at Macy's despite having just come home after serving nine years and seven months in prison, but my friends and associates got fired due to background checks, although I was the person in charge of hiring and firing. My only conclusion is that God opened a door for me that no man could touch. As a result, I consider myself highly blessed. I don't believe in coincidences in my journey. This perspective continues to fuel me, even in my darkest moments, because I understand that nothing happens without the grace of God. It takes faith to walk through those doors and receive blessings.

Seeing so many people still in the same negative mindset motivated me to reach another level of normality in my community. After leaving Macy's, I went to work for Jim Brown, the former NFL player who was one of the key people who put together a gang ceasefire on the Westside of Los Angeles. This ceasefire was able to stop a lot of bloodshed and violence. So, my journey has been blessed. I know that God prepared me for that work by putting me inside those walls so later I could go to the battlefield and reach the people that those in the pulpit can't.

I understand now that my calling was to be in prison at that specific time in my life, so I could learn what I needed to know and come out and fulfill my purpose. Life is all about choices.

While in prison, I chose to educate myself and study diligently. Instead of engaging in negative behavior, I read and learned about various subjects, from the dictionary to Swahili, to my culture and history. I did this without distractions like television or other people around me.

This is the reason why I am where I am today.

Forgiveness

As I humbly share my thoughts and ideas, I understand the importance of forgiving those who wronged us on our journey. It's a two-way street because I wouldn't be where I am today without others forgiving me for wronging them. That's why forgiveness and repentance are key. We need forgiveness in our hearts and ask for God's forgiveness to grow and to understand where we are on our journey.

It's not enough to ask for forgiveness and move on. It's crucial that I make significant changes to ensure that I'm not living the same destructive lifestyle that I once did. I need to actively work on changing my habits and actions, ensuring that they align with my desire to lead a positive and fulfilling life. Only then can I truly move forward from my past mistakes and strive toward a better future.

So, the key to understanding the power of forgiveness is ensuring that I don't repeat the same mistakes I ask for forgiveness for. If something happens once, it's a mistake, but if it happens twice, it becomes a habit. I don't want negative behaviors to become a part of my makeup and reflect poorly on my character. I was raised well, to have a genuine heart, and I stand by that. I want to apologize to anyone on my journey if I have ever caused harm or disrespected you. It's important for me to seek forgiveness and make a conscious effort to change my behavior and habits going forward.

Please forgive me to the highest level of forgiveness. Some people may be able to forgive me, while others may not, and I understand and respect that. If they do forgive me, I am grateful. If not, I trust that God will guide us on our journey and align us so we can come to a sense of giving back and showing compassion for others. I have worked hard to change my thinking from negative to positive and become an asset to my community. Please forgive my past ignorance for any wrongs or harm I have committed.

God's Grace

Being prepared to accept God's grace is crucially important. As the saying goes, "Many are called, but few are chosen." *Therefore, to receive blessings and not succumb to negative thinking, it's crucial to prepare ourselves to become better individuals and strive toward the level of success we aim to achieve.*

To achieve success and avoid a victim mentality, preparing ourselves and working hard toward our goals is an important process. For instance, if I aspire to become a doctor or a lawyer, I need to invest eight years of my life in college to gain the necessary skills and knowledge. We must make sure that we are prepared to receive God's blessings. It's not enough to ask for God's help and expect everything to fall into our laps. We must put in the effort and work hard to achieve our goals.

It's important to recognize our strengths and weaknesses and the positives and negatives in our lives. We can't expect something to come from nothing. We must ensure that our hearts and minds are aligned to receive our blessings. Our thoughts, beliefs, and actions are all interconnected. Setting worthwhile, attainable, and timely goals and using the decision-making process to eliminate the negative and choose the best options is essential. These intangibles help us prepare ourselves to receive God's grace. We must establish a system that works for us, is conducive to our growth and success, and puts us in a position to receive blessings. Remember, a self-fulfilling prophecy results from our thoughts and actions. We must strive toward greatness by putting in the necessary work.

It's important to align our thoughts and beliefs with taking action to achieve our desired outcomes. Of course, we must have faith in ourselves and God's plan for us, but we must also take responsibility for our success.

Remember to set clear and achievable goals, make informed decisions, and take action towards those goals. Let's eliminate negative thinking, establish the facts, and choose our best options. Let's build a system that works for us and puts us in a position to receive blessings. With hard work, dedication, and faith, we can reach the level of greatness that we are meant to achieve.

It's not enough to ask for something and expect it to happen without doing the necessary work. God hears our prayers but also allows us to make choices and act. The difference between those who succeed and those who don't lies in their mental fortitude, their ability to persevere through challenges and attain success. Therefore, it's important to always be prepared, to walk the path of righteousness, and to strive for greatness.

We are the creators of our destiny, shaping our lives and the characters around us based on our beliefs. Our belief system must align with our efforts, requiring us to understand the process, prepare ourselves, establish systems, work hard, and persevere to reach our goals. We control our environment and the outcomes of our lives by our beliefs and actions. Push forward toward success and make a positive impact in the world.

Achieving success is not a great secret or something reserved only for the well-educated or wealthy elite. It's about developing a desire for success and taking action to make it happen. Success is available for anyone who wants it, plans it, and tries to achieve it. Reflect on this and strive toward a path of success.

Part 2: My Community

A Home Needs Two Parents

The development of children thrives when they have both a mother and father in the household. *A child must be raised with both parents present, so he or she can learn and comprehend what it means to be a man or woman.* A mother cannot teach a son how to be a man, just as a father cannot teach a daughter what it means to be a woman. In today's capitalist society, raising a child as a single parent can be difficult, especially with the rich-poor divide widening. I know firsthand the impact of having both parents present in a child's life. After being incarcerated, I came home and married my oldest son's mother. It was one of the most significant things that changed my life. While in prison, I was determined not to allow my son to grow up without a father like me, which I felt was partly responsible for my incarceration.

We eventually separated and divorced after he was raised, but his mother and I maintain a great relationship. We understand that it takes two parents to raise a child, and even more than that, it takes a community. As parents, we need to make sure to have open communication and a clear understanding. The same holds for my daughter's mother. We also maintain a great relationship. I remain present in my children's lives, and there is nothing they go through that I am not a part of since returning home.

It's important to me that my children see the support that they have and know that their father is always there for them. This presence encourages them and instills a sense of worth, belonging, and culture. These elements are missing in many communities, including a solid family structure. When mom and dad are no longer together, children suffer the most, and it's unfair because they didn't cause the situation. Therefore, when bringing a child into the world, both parents should be present to raise the child. It's important to take care of our children emotionally, not just financially, as time spent with them is more valuable than money. Imagine how much better a child's life can be when they have the support of both parents.

My Mother, My Queen

My mother worked two jobs to provide for our family. She was hardworking, and I am grateful for everything she did for us. She instilled the values that have made me who I am today. As a young boy, I played baseball and football. My mother supported me by attending my games and paying for my equipment. Although my athletic pursuits did not work out, my mother's support and encouragement have stayed with me.

My journey has taken me in many different directions, but my mother has always been there to support me. I believe that God has placed me in a situation where I can positively impact the world, and my mother prepared me for this journey.

Growing up without a father was difficult, but my mother's support made it easier. Although my record has caused me difficulties, I have dedicated myself to giving back to my community and helping others. In defining the makeup of a person, I believe that our characteristics are formed by our environment and experiences. I have learned that it takes a village to raise a child and that we all play a part in our community. Therefore, we should give each other credit and appreciate each other's contributions.

Accepting life's changes is important. We should embrace change and be willing to grow. It is important to be comfortable with ourselves and to accept the direction that God gives us. When God removes something from our lives, it is not rejection but direction.

My journey has been shaped by my mother's support and the values she instilled in me. I believe that God has placed me in a position to positively impact the world, and I am grateful for the opportunities that have come my way. It is important to remember that we are all part of a larger community and should appreciate and support each other.

Part 3: My Faith

Struggles and Sacrifices on the Journey
Today is another opportunity for me to bless people's lives with thoughts and perspectives. My journey has been full of struggles, sacrifices, and successes. *Sacrifice is an understatement for most people, and I couldn't always understand the burden I placed on my family.* Although I have no regrets about where I am now, God prepared me for something greater than I ever thought I could achieve. I understand now that my purpose is to journey through God's grace and fulfill his prophecy for me.

I wake up every morning as a vessel, knowing my light will shine through his greatness and sacrifices. At the end of my trek, I hope people understand that I was never a bad person but someone who wanted to be the best under the circumstances presented to me. I apologize from the bottom of my heart for the harm I caused others and their families. I know that no man is perfect, and we all fall short of God's glory at some point.

God has put a glass house around me, and I will carry out the legacy he has planned for me. I take my responsibility of being chosen very seriously. The struggles continue, but I will continue to build and grow.

Greatness lies in the hands of those who prepare themselves for it through work, efforts, and surrounding themselves with people of greatness.

Sacrifice is about giving up a part of myself for the betterment of someone else's gain. Giving up something now for a greater gain later is also a sacrifice. I have had to sacrifice my own selfish pleasures for the betterment of my community, people, and family. I know that everything happens for a reason, and coaching Little League football has been a huge part of that reason. I have created a sports camp to build student-athletes, and I'm proud to see some former students become successful young adults.

If I had to give advice about making a sacrifice, it's a great thing. We should continue to sacrifice and be a vessel that God has chosen. That's where our true blessings come from. I have not been perfect, and I have caused harm. But going back to the negative lifestyle of living the gang culture, I have reconciled the harm I caused and worked to make amends.

I look back from when I was incarcerated to studying and educating myself and then now to where I am, being a vessel, walking the same walks as Martin, Malcolm, Jim, Brother Aquil, and many other pioneers. I'm blessed to have another opportunity to correct my mistakes. But, if we are falling short of God's glory, of our calling, we should do more introspection, ask for forgiveness, and be open to corrections.

I am not perfect, but I have made a difference in my community, for my people, my peers, and my family. Coaching Little League football has been a huge part of that. Being able to help kids who didn't have the opportunity to play and pay for their expenses has been my calling. I want to show my people, peers, and family that it takes a village to get to a higher level and help others. I have also helped create a fourteen-gang ceasefire in Los Angeles, saving many lives.

My purpose is to give back, to be a product of change, to effect social change, and to make amends through my work. I will continue to be a vessel that God has chosen, and I hope to leave a positive legacy at the end of my journey.

Accountability and Glass Houses

I am a humble traveler, journeying through life by the grace of God's will and doing his work to fulfill my destiny. My soul is devoted to God, and my exterior is just a small reflection of God's greater purpose for me. Yet, as I observe my fellow companions, I see many living false lives, chasing empty dreams and destinies. My mission is to reach out to lost people and bring them to the truth. *It's not about where you're from, but where you're at.*

We are all equal in the eyes of God, and we are all part of the same human race. Through God's guidance, we can grow and develop our unique growth opportunities. As members of our community, it's important that we hold ourselves accountable and reflect on the values we want to pass on to future generations.

I don't judge others; instead, I share my journey and experiences with an open heart and mind. I've learned that what we put into our journey is what we'll get out of it. I understand that opposing forces want to see me fail, but I have faith in God and trust in the journey that he has set out for me.

At times, I reflect on my progress and ask myself, "Where do we go from here?" I've been able to hold myself and others accountable, and I strive to continue doing so. Everyone has a purpose in our community, and it's important that we find and fulfill that purpose.

The journey toward defining one's legacy is a challenging process, but it's also an opportunity for growth and self-discovery. It requires faith, perseverance, and a willingness to face the unknown. We must learn to appreciate the journey and trust in the process, brick by brick and step by step. We need to set goals, make plans, and understand that failure is part of the process.

As we progress on our journey, we must build a strong relationship with God and listen to our inner spirit. We must trust that God has a plan for us and have faith that we are on the right path. The journey can be scary sometimes, but it's important to remember that God will never take us somewhere we are not meant to be. With God's guidance and our efforts, we can continue growing and fulfilling our destiny.

Yesterday's Mistakes are Today's Lessons

I am humbly traveling on my journey, guided by the grace of God's will and fulfilling my destiny by doing His work. My inner being is bared to God, and my exterior is just a small glimpse of what He wants others to see. As I observe those around me striving to live up to false destinies, I work to reach those who have lost their way. My desire is for my people to always remain authentic. *At the end of the day, it's not about where we come from but where we are headed.* We are all equal in the eyes of God, and our journey as humans is to grow and evolve.

Through our actions and words, we can shape the values and messages we impart to the younger generation. I am not here to judge anyone but to share my thoughts and experiences from a place of vulnerability and honesty. I understand that what I put into my journey is what I will receive in return. Although the journey may not always be easy, I have the same opportunities as others if I apply myself. I recognize that opposing forces wish to see me fail, but I also know that I have an advantage because of my faith in God.

As I reflect on my mission, I am grateful for the ability to hold myself and others accountable. Everyone has a purpose in our community, and it is our responsibility to discover and fulfill it. While I don't claim to be a great man, I am a man who understands his calling, and I am committed to fulfilling it. Each day, as I wake up, I am reminded that the struggle continues, and I am constantly learning on my journey.

One of the greatest challenges in life is being honest with oneself. As we strive to define our legacy, we must recognize that self-discovery is a journey of faith. We must learn to trust the process, brick by brick and step by step. The building blocks of our vision must be put in place, and we must work tirelessly to make our dreams a reality. It's important to remember that the journey is just as important as the end goal.

To navigate this journey, we must educate ourselves and build a relationship with God. By doing so, we can hear His inner spirit speaking to us, guiding us toward our destiny. We must be willing to take risks, set goals, and have a plan for achieving them. Along the way, we must be prepared for failure and willing to pick ourselves up and try again. No matter what happens, we must remember that we are worthy in the eyes of God.

We will encounter obstacles and challenges that will test our faith throughout our journey. However, we must trust that God has a plan for us and will never take us anywhere we are not meant to be. Although the journey may be scary, we must learn to appreciate it and cherish the lessons we learn.

Daily Struggles

As I sit here, my heart is heavy, and my thoughts are consumed by the everyday process of discovering my true identity. *The journey of self-discovery is a step-by-step process.* Still, it's essential to understand that we often encounter life situations beyond our control. Therefore, while I encourage everyone to create their own legacies, we must acknowledge those who have helped us along the way. I want to pay homage to God and my mother, who instilled greatness in me and sacrificed so much for me and my family. I strive to leave a legacy that honors their sacrifices.

Reflecting on my life, I realize that everything that happened was designed for me to become who I am today. I dreamed of playing baseball and football as a child, and my mother supported my aspirations. Unfortunately, I made bad choices that led me astray from that path, but I now understand that it wasn't my calling. I speak about setting goals and aspiring to greatness. Still, we must also accept that trial and error is part of the journey, and failure is necessary for growth.

Each day presents a different obstacle, and we must stay vigilant and be ready to face them. We must remember that we are kings and queens on our journey and have a place and purpose in life. Our experiences shape our character, and I define character as someone who stands up for what they believe in, speaks the truth with integrity, and keeps their word.

My character has shaped my journey, which was influenced by my beliefs and upbringing. At seventeen, I was incarcerated but never went back to prison after my release at twenty-seven. I started working. God works in mysterious ways, and I believe everything in my life has been part of his plan.

I was blessed to be offered an opportunity to work for Jim Brown, a Hall of Fame football player. I learned valuable life skills from his Amer-I-Can curriculum. Though I was initially unmotivated, I eventually realized the value of these skills. For ten years, I trained myself to become a better person.

Real talk: we must keep our heads up high, stay blessed, sidestep the weak ones, and know that our day is coming. Life is full of unexpected twists and turns. Still, with faith, hard work, and dedication, we can overcome any obstacle and achieve greatness.

Self-Determination to Build Solid Foundations
While enjoying the view, I contemplate the transition to another level. God has closed some doors but has always opened others. Transitioning is a process that is difficult to comprehend and is out of our control. We have been conditioned to believe that many aspects of transitioning are normal, but this is not necessarily true. Understanding the process of transitioning is crucial, as misunderstandings and confusion can occur without it.

It is important to have a plan and understand the process for a successful transition. It is a period in our lives where we must enjoy the journey and have faith that God will guide us where we are meant to be. *Finding oneself along the way may mean encountering obstacles, but this is part of the journey.* I have realized that looking outside of myself is just as important as introspection. To help others flourish, I need to flourish myself, which means building a solid foundation. Everything is connected, and our purpose is not defined by our mistakes or limitations.

Transitioning to another level means evolving spiritually, mentally, and physically, knowing where we are supposed to be and what we are supposed to do. It involves knowing that our hard work and effort are not coincidental, and we must prepare for it. I have studied the greats who have come before me and aspire to be among their ranks. Self-reflection and introspection are essential in the transition process. It allows us to evaluate ourselves honestly about our accomplishments, setbacks, and goals.

It is a daily growth process that helps us be better fathers, leaders, sons, and students. We must be honest with ourselves on every level and use self-reflection to set attainable and measurable goals. The incentive to transition to the next level comes from the desire to be a beacon of hope for others and a vessel God uses to shed light. We must remember that we are made in God's image, and transitioning to another level is part of His plan.

God aligns the stars at the perfect moment to allow us to hear his voice, discover our purpose, and recognize our greatness. Sometimes, we must remove ourselves from a situation to introspect and gain perspective. We can find answers that may surprise us by looking from the outside. We should be wary of false prophecies and take responsibility for our self-determination. This self-awareness and inner peace empower us to speak out and advocate for those God aligns us with. We should share the message that God is sending us through the challenges that are prerequisites for greater things to come.

As we wait for these greater things, we must trust in God and believe in our abilities. We cannot be complacent in fulfilling our purpose, and we must be willing to step out of our comfort zone and rely on faith. To achieve greatness, we must combine our faith with hard work and set realistic and attainable goals for ourselves. We must be open to growth, learning, and evolution as individuals. Our faith assures us that God will not lead us where we are not meant to be. We must learn to remove distractions and be grateful for God's blessings each day. Waking up each morning is a blessing, and we should recognize that God is still using us to fulfill and bless others. Finally, we must surround ourselves with people who have our best interests at heart and want to see us grow and succeed.

Despite our hardships, we must remember that we are still worthy of serving God. We are a reflection of him, and our journey will shape us into history. So, take a moment to breathe, feel the air, and appreciate the beauty around us. Trust in God's plan, remain grateful, humble, and thankful, and always be willing to listen to his message.

Part 4: The Change

The Conscious Mind

I want to discuss the power of the conscious mind and its ability to recognize correct decisions, thoughts, ideas, and ideologies. When we consider the creative mind, both the conscious and the subconscious are involved, but how do they work, and where do they come from? We focus on the conscious mind when we examine our reactions, beliefs, and self-characteristics. Conversely, the subconscious mind is akin to our heart, and aligning our thoughts is essential to unlocking our potential.

But how can we do that if we are raised in an environment that limits our ability to see beyond our daily world? We must recognize that we are interconnected and shift our thinking to a broader perspective. It starts from the beginning, at birth, when we must understand our purpose and align ourselves with God's purpose. Society and the system have systematically stripped us of our natural selves, including our culture, heritage, and land, making it difficult for us to succeed.

*To build and grow, we must change the lens through which we see ourselves. We must reprogram our minds to become the best versions of ourselves._*Ultimately, we ask ourselves how we can find fulfillment on our journey. To do this, we must focus on the 3 Cs: creation, connection, and contribution. By creating, we unleash our creativity and potential. Through connection, we form meaningful relationships and connections with others. And by making contributions, we leave a positive impact on the world. At the end of the day, our legacy and journey are solely ours to control, but we must first learn our history to understand where we come from and where we are going.

Surround Yourself with the Right People

When I speak about my personal journey, I often emphasize the importance of being around people who are smarter and more successful than me, as they can provide guidance and tools for achieving my goals. *Conversely, being around negative people who engage in destructive behavior can hinder my progress and potentially lead me down a destructive path.* It's essential to remember that not everyone can grow with me on my journey, and that's okay.

Although it may seem straightforward to eliminate negative influences, it can be challenging because it often requires letting go of past relationships and situations that no longer serve my best interests. Suppose I want to make a positive impact on my community. In that case, I need to surround myself with people who share similar values and want to see me succeed. It's important to remain humble and open to learning from others, regardless of background or age. By setting goals and holding myself accountable, I can measure my progress and ensure that I continually grow and evolve.

Success requires hard work and determination, and while inspiration can be a helpful starting point, it's the ninety percent of perspiration that leads to tangible results. By surrounding myself with the right people, staying focused, and being disciplined, I can achieve what I envision in my mind and positively impact those around me.

Controlling the Narrative

The topic of slavery weighs heavily on my mind, especially the situations that have arisen from it. Slavery has played a significant role in defining legacies and perpetuating racism. It is a product of one group of individuals dominating and controlling another group's narrative. The question is whether this stems from the dominant group's insecurities or their greed. Through our journey of understanding the effects of slavery on people, can the dominant group still call themselves Christians? Are events like the Holocaust, the Iraq War, and the oppression of the people of Iran similar, where one group controls the narrative while the other suffers? These events seem intertwined, as if they must be in place to control things by the powers.

Slavery runs deep into our psyche and has played a major part in the lack of growth of many different urban communities. By "urban communities," I refer to a state of mind and place where people struggle to survive and fight for resources. We put the poor on welfare and make them dependent on the dominant group, which still covertly controls the narrative. There are many subtle mechanisms still being used to control. For instance, a teacher I spoke to had students from different races and had to work hard to prove that she had their best interests at heart.

We live in a society where one ethnicity has to prove they are not a bigot or racist when interacting with another race. *There is only one race, the human race, and many dynamics occur daily.* The point goes back to slavery and how it affects every person today. It allows the controllers to keep pitting us against each other for profit. Remember, knowledge is power, and we are all God's children. To stop being controlled, we must understand that we are all brothers and sisters, not enemies.

Part 5: Finding Myself

My Ideology

My view of the world is one of purpose and compassion for the community. I understand that I must go through adverse situations and circumstances to have revelation and help others grow. My purpose is to realize that I am a man of God. I am a man that did not get to choose my faith and my calling. God prepared me for something I didn't know would be necessary for my present day. *My ideology about the world is for us to be put in situations to uplift our people, to show our people that there's only one way to unite a community; being human with one race: the human race.*

My purpose is to show we're all connected and spiritually divine under one universal law and that there is good and evil in all situations. We must distinguish what is good and bad for us and apply what is good to the world. I often speak about Martin Luther King and Malcolm X. Why do I bring those two individuals up? I discuss them to show the similarities and differences between them and myself. Martin, a brother raised in the South, was put in a situation on his journey where he didn't understand his calling. He had a gift from God to speak, unite, organize, and teach. These are qualities that I possess.

I am a man of strong values, discipline, loyalty, and integrity. Malcolm was a guy who came from street life, went to prison, studied, educated himself, and came home and fulfilled his calling. He did not know he would be one of the top leaders in the United States and would unite our people. I share a similar parallel with Malcolm. I was a guy who underwent a process when I went to jail. I, studied and became educated. I went through the dictionary, from aardvark to the end, and learned to speak Swahili.

Then, I came home and spoke to my family about what I had learned. This experience changed me, and I began my journey of community intervention.

I have been blessed to travel to Miami with Aquil Basheer, a community intervention leader, to speak about public policy and to Washington D.C. to conduct training in community-based public safety.

These experiences were spiritually connecting to me. They made me understand that I share some of the same prophecies, and I know now that my calling is to sacrifice for my people, to be a light in a dark place.

I understand now that God reversed the curse. He sent me through a dark place early in my journey to now be a beacon of light, change, and hope for our people and our community. So, I often reference Martin and Malcolm because I share some of their ideologies.

I've been through some of the same situations they've gone through, and I share the same struggle, and the battle helps us win. I know I'm just a vessel God uses to continue carrying on the legacy.

Finding My Legacy

I feel compelled to speak about revelations during the darkest hours when we are alone. How honest are we with ourselves when it comes to defining our legacy? Do we talk the talk, or do we walk the walk? Do we struggle with things that are within our control? In my own life, I have faced many challenges and have gone through difficult situations. God has guided me to reveal myself not as I want others to see me but from a place of truth that I often see reflected in the mirror. *As I share my perspective, trying to be as honest and authentic as possible, I realize that my legacy is my understanding of myself.* It means living my life in truth and defining myself by my legacy. Many people struggle similarly to me, and I often have moments of revelation about my legacy when speaking to people about their struggles.

God blessed me and allowed me to travel worldwide to have those moments of revelation, making me feel like Malcolm X when he traveled to Mecca and came back with a different perspective. We cannot criticize him for trying to find his legacy because he was raised in a society that taught him to think a certain way about himself.

It is our time for revelation, for change from the things we have gone through and situations we have placed ourselves in. We often talk about struggling to understand where and who we are. Still, every day is a struggle, and we face different challenges every day. I know God has placed me where I'm supposed to be when I'm supposed to be. I now understand that every action was a reaction based on my experiences. I have learned that my legacy is to remain steadfast in my truth and help others understand my experiences in a way that helps them. At the end of the day, I have to look at myself in the mirror alone and live the truth of my experiences. I want to adhere to and fulfill my legacy. I've been taught to understand and fulfill the prophecy that is right for me.

Every day, I still struggle with finding myself, but I understand that only I can define my legacy, and only God can bless me based on what I do, not what I say. I will live my legacy and make sure that I fulfill it for my family, friends, and all those around me. If you ever see, but don't really see me, yet hear me speak, it will be my truth. When I speak, know that I speak from a place of truth.

My legacy is to be a humble, strong father and leader who understands that the journey is not about me. I stand for change and understand that my mistakes have given me a testimony to speak. I adhere to truth and make sure that I act with integrity. I have not been perfect. I have faced challenges and had forks on the road. Succumbing to the lifestyle of negativity that was prevalent in my community contributed to those challenges.

Reflecting on my journey, I want to be remembered as someone who overcame his struggles and lived a life of integrity and honesty, positively impacting those around me.

Evolving to Understand Destiny
Evolving into our true selves means understanding the growth and development of our path, which allows us to make mistakes and learn from them. Recognizing this opportunity for growth lets us know that we are on a blessed path guided by God. *Through experience, we learn what good, bad, and in-between is. We must evaluate the things in the middle and determine if they will help us evolve or make us stagnant.* We ask ourselves, "Am I evolving to where God wants me to be, or am I just a

reflection of what I see? Am I a product of my environment?"

I've learned that to grow, I needed to understand my weaknesses and what I lacked in skills. I had to accept that I haven't created answers for everything and that there are things in my destiny that have not yet come to pass. Self-evolution is a day-to-day journey, and I still struggle with it. I ask myself, "Should I kill my struggles or grow them into something different?"

Growing up in a community of gangs and drugs, I became a product of my environment. The people, places, and things around me formed my habits and beliefs. As a result, I needed to eliminate negative people in my life and surround myself with those with my best interests at heart.

Despite experiencing the lows and highs of life, I am still evolving on my journey. I have had time to reflect on my legacy and path while sitting behind prison walls for nine years and seven months. I never saw myself as a victim but as someone who believes that God put me where I needed to be to become reflective, grow, and evolve.

Destiny holds great value and meaning because it is my daughter's middle name. It was meant to manifest, and I put hard work and effort into it. Further growth and development mean being a student who evolves and seeks answers, truth, and righteousness daily.

The Race of Life

I have experienced moments of self-discovery where I hoped for certain things. Still, obstacles arose, leading me down different paths. Despite setbacks, my faith in God has sustained me, and I'm grateful for the blessings that have come my way. It took years of asking for guidance, but I trusted that God would reveal my destiny when I was ready.

My journey has been one of growth, with moments of uncertainty, shame, and mistakes. However, I continue to evolve and manifest my belief system daily, putting in the necessary work to realize my destiny. I have learned that preparation, study, and isolation from distractions are key to following the right path.

Coaching Little League football for two decades has been a great success in my life. It has been rewarding to see the same kids I coached making it to the NFL or leading fulfilling lives with their families. But the fact that I have helped change someone's life for the better is the greatest reward for me.

As a father, I am committed to being present in my kids' lives, and I ensure they know I will never disappoint them. I take full accountability for my actions and have learned from past mistakes. We must all strive to be proactive and control what we can before pointing fingers and blaming others. Accountability is crucial in our journey. *Learning how to receive my destiny was life changing. As a result, I was ready when good things came my way, and I will continue to evolve and grow as a person.*

Each person's journey is unique and personal. A journey of self-discovery and growth through our efforts and hard work leads us to say, "I have arrived." But when we do arrive, we must ask ourselves: what challenges will we face next? Arriving means understanding our journey, including that society often categorizes and labels us. Society can build us up or tear us down, but we must hold ourselves accountable.

It's important to recognize that false perceptions can distort our understanding of ourselves and our environment. For example, we may ask ourselves if we are simply products of our surroundings. Still, we must also remember that every action has a reaction, and every trial has an error. The journey is equally valuable whether we run 100 yards or a marathon. The length of our journey does not determine its worth or impact. Regardless of the length of their journey, every person has an important story to tell.

Along the way, we learn that we are not perfect. We make mistakes, but using these hurdles as opportunities to overcome obstacles and grow is important. We must define who we are and the legacy we want to leave. It is about doing what is right and treating others how we want to be treated on our journey. We cannot look to others to fulfill our destiny or blame them for our shortcomings. Only we and God can determine our path and legacy.

Remember that mistakes do not define us. We may stumble or fall short, but that does not make us less of an individual. We must keep moving forward on our journey with God's guidance. Immediate gratification may be tempting, but hard work and dedication will lead us to greatness. God blesses us all on our journey.

Everyone Has a Voice, and Every Voice Deserves to be Heard

We are all unique individuals God created with distinct personalities and abilities. Each of us has the potential to create a legacy that reflects our unique strengths and perspectives. If we conform to societal norms and expectations, we may miss out on opportunities to grow and become leaders and teachers ourselves. Labels and titles only define us when we allow our actions and accomplishments to give them meaning. Therefore, it's crucial to cultivate an image of self-worth, respect, dignity, and honesty.

God made us all different for a reason. It's essential to embrace our individuality and nurture our talents so we can blossom into the person God intended us to be. Sometimes, we may feel pressure to follow in someone else's footsteps or conform to their expectations. However, we must resist this urge and embrace our unique path in life.

It's crucial for everyone to have a voice because each of us brings a valuable perspective to the table. We should encourage others to speak up and share their knowledge and experiences to help us grow and learn. *When we allow everyone to have a say and flourish in their own time, we create an environment of growth and learning.*

Remember that there are no big "I's" or little "you's" in this journey of life. We are all valuable and have something to contribute. Don't let anyone make you feel like your voice doesn't matter. Your experiences and knowledge could be what someone else needs to hear to learn and grow.

Ask yourself "What is your goal?" What is controlling the narrative?" Think about one's longevity in the response and not focus on immediate gratification. What is the short-term goal? How many steps to get to your purpose (that is your long-term goal). Stay focused and driven. Goals must be realistic and worthwhile for what you obtain. If not, they are a distraction. Eliminate the negative and establish facts to focus on. Stay disciplined and consistent. It takes mental determination and fortitude. If I reflected on these thoughts this way, I would not have shortened my life's purpose and lost time.

Disruption to Be Heard

Why do men often need to be loud and disruptive to be heard? No one acknowledges my existence or hears me out. *Allowing people, particularly men, to share their thoughts and experiences provides an outlet and relatability.* But why do I feel like no one hears me when I speak? Is it because my demeanor is too loud that my words get lost? My demeanor reflects the characteristics I was taught: to be strong and dominant in a world that values the powerful and disregards the weak. But my demeanor is not a deflection; it is a reflection of many others like me. We are not beasts of destruction but creatures looking for a better way. We need to tame ourselves in an untamed society. We live in a dog-eat-dog world with dog-eat-dog people, but we do not have to subscribe to dog-eat-dog ideologies.

Despite being well-respected and listened to in my community, no one believes me or takes my problems seriously when I am going through something myself. This can be frustrating, especially as a productive Black man who can lead companies and create generational wealth for my family. Everyone needs to be heard, especially the underprivileged, who often have no voice. When we are not heard, it can lead to triggers and generational trauma.

It is important to listen to others when they speak and be honest when asked how we are doing. Complaining does not solve anything, but being heard is valuable and necessary. God gave us two ears and one mouth for a reason, to listen more than we talk. Listen to your subconscious and inner being, and trust what you hear and feel.

My demeanor includes my beliefs, characteristics, body language, and appearance. I know my demeanor speaks loudly because I have a serious look. It conveys a "no nonsense" attitude, honesty, loyalty, and dedication to social change. I want to be seen as a stand-up guy who has overcome obstacles and can be an example in my community. But achieving this takes hard work, dedication, and commitment. We must strive for it because commitment changes our mindset, drive, and focus.

Living in an unruly society that is always changing, we must proceed cautiously, learn triggers, remove threats, and defuse bad situations. If we cannot defuse a situation, we must safely remove ourselves. We must also look at specific societies of unruliness, find out their needs, and see if we can help address their situations with resources and solutions.

To not subscribe to a dog-eat-dog society we should stop watching negative news, close our eyes, and listen to limited resources and opportunities. Bias is high in environments with few opportunities to succeed, and competition can breed an environment of conflict. But as humans, we can change our thinking and navigate through difficult situations.

Part 6: Here and Now

I Can't Believe I Am Here

It's hard to believe that I am where I am today, doing the work that I'm doing and reflecting on how much my journey has changed. I feel blessed to have the opportunity to share my story and inspire others. I never thought I would speak on panels, create podcasts, and advocate for change nationwide. I'm grateful that God has given me this platform to be a voice for hope and positivity.

I want to encourage others to never abandon their dreams and keep searching for greatness. We all have the power to create change and positively impact the world. *Focusing on what you can control and being the best at what you do is important.* Trust in yourself and have faith that the future holds great things.

I went through the Amer-I-Can program at Jim Brown's house. Then, some of my friends brought in other people from different neighborhoods, and we really put out some of the fires of war raging since the early eighties. It was not just me but my community backing me that made it happen. To this day, the ceasefire is still in place.

Am I Heading in The Right Direction?
As a community, we must control the narrative shaping our identity and future. We can do this through collaborative efforts, such as the Professional Community Intervention Training Institute (PCITI) and other prevention agencies and vested community-based organizations (CBOs).

Through these alliances, we can identify common problems and develop solutions tailored to each community's unique needs. *We can create planned systems, build templates, and ensure that all members of our communities are accounted for and understand their roles in shaping our collective destiny.*

Changing the mindset of our community is crucial in this effort. We must educate, retrain, and restructure our processes and systems, including our educational system, media consumption, and cultural output. By controlling the narrative from all perspectives and walks of life, we can ensure that our communities become products of our positive environments.

It is important to remember that we are not powerless; we have the power to change our communities for the better. By taking control of the narrative and empowering ourselves, we can increase our power and create a brighter future for all.

Part 7: Words for the Future Generations

Build Slowly

When it comes to achieving greatness, a process must take place. *Building slowly with knowledge and wisdom is a crucial part of that process.* Looking at the world around us, we can see that nothing of true value was created overnight. Rome was not built in a day, and neither are our lives.

To become who we are designed to be, we must start from a seed and be nurtured and watered to develop into our raw essence. Along our journey, it's important to prepare ourselves rightfully and not get caught up in worldly distractions that can take our focus away. We must work hard to obtain and sustain what we want for a long time instead of rushing to get it and losing it quickly.

However, building slowly doesn't mean living a lesser life or having less value. Every life has its own journey and value, no matter how long or short. Someone may obtain and retain information faster than others, but they still need to build slowly.

To build effectively, we must create a system that allows us to build mechanisms and operations that govern the process. So, take your time to build slowly, but take advantage of your blessings. When we move too fast, we can miss important things. We must slow down and retrace our steps to see what's around us. Patience is a virtue. Building slowly with knowledge and wisdom is important to achieve greatness and longevity.

Generational Wealth

When we examine the current times, going back to the Rockefellers and the Morgans, and a few other families that control much of the world and country today, we see how their families are financially set for life without having to do much more than maintain their wealth. *In contrast, those without generational wealth have a different mindset, becoming more desperate and hungrier. That needs to change.* Their drive and work ethic differ from those who have had everything handed to them.

Creating generational wealth for one's children and their descendants is critical, as it establishes systems of success, operational procedures, guidelines, and structures that transcend generations. These systems enable families and communities to create and maintain economic stability for a long time. It is essential to be mindful that the steps taken now are prerequisites for future generations, ensuring they can create systems that provide economic stability.

We need to control the narrative, own what we invest in, and spend money on every day. Investing in ourselves and our spending habits is vital for creating generational wealth. For example, investing in businesses like Starbucks, PlayStation, and McDonald's can be wise since we spend our money on them daily. This tip is part of a broader understanding that generational wealth is linked to survival tools, mechanisms, credit, and financial literacy. Take care of your credit and only burn through your resources with an understanding of their value.

Yesterday's Mistakes are Today's Blessings

For me to create a level of peace and unity within my tribe and community, I had to ask myself how I was able to do that. *Looking back on my childhood, I realized that I needed someone who looked like me and could relate to receive information and effect change.*

It's important to understand that yesterday's mistakes can lead to today's blessings. Without going through the challenges I've faced, I wouldn't have the understanding and knowledge I do now. History has shown us that people who have made mistakes and failed their way to success have laid the foundation for us to follow and achieve our goals.

Everything in life starts from a negative and builds into a positive. It's like planting a seed. If it's watered and nurtured, it will grow. Making mistakes is a part of the journey, and we shouldn't be afraid of them. We must step out on faith and learn from our mistakes to master our strengths and overcome our weaknesses.

However, it's important to correct our mistakes and not let them become habits or decisions that work against us. By learning from our mistakes, we can use them to work for our good instead of our detriment.

Lead with the Right Intentions

Seeking validation from others can be a tricky thing. We all need to lead with the right intentions and ensure that our work is pure, done out of a desire for truth and righteousness, and not just for personal gain. *While validation from our people and tribe is important because we represent them daily, it's equally important to not rely on external validation for our motivation.* Our calling is not about us, but rather, our work is for someone else's gain.

It's essential to lead with the right intent, ensuring that our actions are driven by the desire to see others win and not by the expectation of personal gain. While it's natural to want validation from our tribe, it's equally vital to avoid seeking validation for our work. It should come from a place of truth and righteousness, not incentives. As vessels of knowledge, we are here to serve others, and our work should be focused on their gain rather than ours.

Validation is critical, but we must ensure that we lead correctly, as we are products of our community. It's not about seeking praise but acknowledging our positive impact in our communities. Let's be accountable for our actions and strive to make a meaningful change that will benefit others. In this way, we can channel the frequencies aligned in the universe and transcend through every moment of growth and evolution.

Never Give Up

On my journey, I've had moments where I felt like giving up. For example, after fighting a case for three years and knowing I wasn't guilty, I felt exhausted and drained, like all the energy and air had been sucked out of me. I was in a losing battle and felt nobody was listening to me. Many people go through similar experiences because we bottle up so much and don't get a chance to talk or be heard.

But know that you're not alone. There's always someone going through something worse than you. Keep the faith and stay prayed up, knowing that God hears us and won't place us anywhere we're not supposed to be.

If God places us somewhere, there's a lesson to be learned.

There's a creative solution for every obstacle, so channel your inner scholar and always be a student in the game. Life throws us challenges and tests to see how strong we are and what phase of life we're in. Everything we go through is a test and an opportunity for growth and evolution.

There are two great moments in a man or woman's life: when we're born and understand our purpose. *We'll never understand our purpose if we give up on our journey.* When you feel like quitting, think about the challenges you've already overcome and how they've made you stronger.

Our ancestors and forefathers would have quit their dreams, and we wouldn't be where we are today if they had. You have so much to give to the world, so many thoughts and ideas inside your head that God has instilled in you. Don't give up on your journey.

What Does the Future Look Like

I envision a community where people live in harmony and view each other as friends, not foes. It is a community where individuals have opportunities to provide for their families and lead a comfortable life. Additionally, it is a community where there is peace in the universe. This includes peace, love, unity, and respect. However, the system and status quo often hinder our happiness and success.

We need to analyze our environment and ask ourselves why we have one of the wealthiest countries in the world but also one of the largest homeless populations. These issues were created by systems that were supposed to be sustainable but instead work against us. We must take control of the narrative and hold our city councils and mayors accountable.

Our community leaders must ensure that our communities are safe to live in, minimize violence, and increase educational opportunities. We need to create jobs and systems that allow individuals to thrive. A perfect world would involve truth instead of lies and deception that control our narrative, leading to a state of crisis. We need to tell our stories from the eyes of those who feel the story. We need to help people deal with their mental health and PTSDs, as wounded people tend to hurt others. *In summary, a beautiful world is one with equality and peace.*

About the Author

Tommie "Ttop" Rivers
An individual committed to restoring peace to traumatized and violent-prone communities, Mr. Rivers has re-dedicated his life to community restoration. He is an abundance of positivity in the lives of youth and young adults he touches. He is not only a member of the phenomenal Instructional and Leadership Team of P.C.I.T.I, but he also coaches, speaks, and gives every bit of himself to his community and those in need.

About the Editors

Sonya Carey, M.S.
Sonya Carey is a former foster youth and foster care advocate. She is a recent graduate and part of the first cohort for the Master of Science in Hospitality and Tourism Management at USC. She is the author of *Make It or Bake It: Recipes for Transitioning Foster Youth*. Ms. Carey has been working in food service for more than 15 years and has worked as a food service manager for LAUSD and Chicago Public Schools. Currently, she is working as Administrative Services Director and Academic Coordinator for Dr. Debra LLC, helping to lead human resources efforts and build academic courses at the Listen and Love University.

Debra Warner, Psy.D.
Dr. Debra Warner is a Full Professor and CEO/President of Dr. Debra Publishing LLC. Her areas of expertise include: male survivors related to trauma and violence, community gang intervention, immigration and mental health, competency, psychological testing, diversity, personality disorders, and substance abuse. Dr. Warner is a frequent speaker at conferences and other venues and has given a TedX Talk, as well as appearing on CBS. She is involved in social media and is an oft-quoted expert in books, television and radio.